The Great Soccer Guide for First Time Coaches…and Beyond

Coaching Fun, Healthy, Successful Youth Soccer for Coaches Who Never Played the Game

By Rick Gordon, PhD.

TABLE OF CONTENTS

Introduction

This book aims to give new coaches a concise and useful guide that imparts an appreciation of the sport, clarifies the purposes for youth sports, and offers easy to follow advice for organizing practices and coaching games for youth, all while keeping a perspective that encourages development of youth as good people and good players.

Like everyone else of my generation playing soccer, I started when Pele', the greatest player of all time, came to the United States to play for the New York Cosmos in the old North American Soccer League (NASL). I was about 12 and not a very coordinated kid. I couldn't make the team in more traditional sports like basketball, but soccer was unpopular enough back then that I don't think they cut anyone from the team. After a couple years of minimal playing time, I improved by attending some soccer camps and was able to make the high school varsity in 11th grade (although I was still part of the "Turtle Sprints" among the slowest on the team). I practiced a lot in the off-season with a friend, but still played only sporadically for the high school team. Somehow, over the summer before starting college, I became faster and more coordinated and when I went off to Stanford University, I walked on to tryouts and played four years of varsity soccer there. We were ranked in the top 20 nationally, went to NCAA playoffs, and I was a starter for three years at one of the best soccer programs in the country.

I continued to play on adult teams and while in graduate school, I was selected to play for the Minnesota Strikers development team in the NASL. I continue to play at age 55, with a wonderful group of 40+ year olds from all over the world that can still beat college teams by playing within our limits, enjoying each other's company, and being really shrewd about where we expend our energy.

Along the way, I have gotten a PhD in Education, taught high school, founded a charter middle and high school, led international travel programs, traveled around the world for a year with my wife and kids, and taught and coached learners at all age levels in all sorts of areas.

I have seen lots of great coaches in my time, and sadly, have seen even more bad ones. I have been running our local youth soccer program for 6 years, making soccer fun for kids from age 5-12 and conscientiously staying out of the competitive local league that seemed to have too many games, too much travel, and too many players on the field to assure the kids would enjoy the game and be involved in the way I wanted each of them to be. This past season, with the kids I started with now near middle school age, we finally joined the 5th-6th grade league, winning everything from the league championship to any tournament we entered (although we always had the youngest team by far, including several 3rd and 4th graders in what is a 6th grade league).

Most disappointingly, I see parents who are good hearted, volunteering countless hours to help coach youth soccer but having little sense of what to do to make this a positive experience for the kids. I see coaches and parents on the sidelines yelling at kids, trying to direct every movement of the players. I see too many teams where one or two kids have the ball most of the time while everyone else stands around and watches. I see kids in lines, waiting to do drills where a couple kids are moving and everyone else is standing watching. I see kids neither learning about soccer nor having a whole lot of fun. And most troubling, I see all this being done with a big focus on winning, and at least when they play our team, the opposing team is not even getting that satisfaction.

I think there is a better way. As I try to convey here, there are probably several goals of youth sports—physical fitness, teamwork, personal growth, skill development, goal setting, sportsmanship, friendship, fun. Winning is surely one of these goals, but I contend that when you emphasize winning, you almost surely miss out on the other goals. If you do well on the other goals, my experience has been, you do pretty well with the winning. And as a parent and coach, I know everyone is happier when the kids are learning and growing and having fun, and on top of all that, they are winning too.

Chapter 1: The Beautiful Game

La Jugo Bonita--The Beautiful Game. The starting point for coaching youth soccer is to understand the beauty of the sport. This can be a challenge for American adults raised on the big three American sports of football, baseball, and basketball. Yet soccer is by far the world's most popular sport, drawing over half the world's population to watch the World Cup Final and being played by 1.6 billion people worldwide.

In some ways, soccer is closer to theater than sport. From the line-up of teams and referees before the game to the exchange of jerseys and bows to the fans at the end, soccer is an art and a drama that can capture all life's emotions in the space of a game.

The distinguishing trait of soccer is it is a game that flows. Unlike football with stoppages after every play, or baseball with its strikes and balls and outs and innings, or even basketball with timeouts and fouls shots, soccer is all about flow. At the professional level, the game proceeds for 45 minutes each half without break. Substitutes are limited and permanent. And the game itself is played all over the field, from end to end, switching in a breath from offense to defense. A team can go from despair to glory in a split second. Fans erupt in joy when their pent up anticipation is released as their team finally finds their way to the goal.

As a youth soccer coach, you needn't appreciate all the intricacies of the game, but it helps to be able to convey the spirit of the game to children, so they can value its most positive characteristics.

What is there to love about soccer? The drama, etiquette, sportsmanship, flow, excitement, creativity, grace, teamwork, physical effort, history, worldwide popularity, and sheer athleticism. Soccer is the world's most popular game, and a soccer player will run 6-10 miles in a game, using every part of the body, great vision, and concentrated thinking for 90 minutes of intensity.

As a soccer player, you can go anywhere in the world and make connections just by pulling out a ball on any street and start playing with your feet. It is truly the international game and may be the one man-made creation that is common to the most people in the world.

The Goals of Youth Soccer

No matter what the age of the kids or what community you live in, the goals for youth soccer are the same—to gain a sense of sportsmanship, teamwork, personal development, physical fitness, skill development, challenging oneself, fun. Somewhere on this list, many people probably put winning, but at best, this falls a bit down the list of priorities. And in fact, as almost every good youth coach can tell you, if you do the first eight things right, winning follows pretty consistently.

Prioritizing winning, however, can easily undermine many of these other goals. If you want to know just how to win at youth soccer, I can give you the plan right here: find the best and fastest one or two players you have, cultivate their talents, and then find some way to get them the ball in games and let them dribble through everyone else to try to score. This will win you many games at younger ages, although it will do almost nothing to develop your other players and even these one or two stars will never learn how to be strong soccer players. That takes vision and teamwork and field sense you can't get from being a one-person team.

A focus on winning can run directly counter to your other goals. Teamwork usually goes out the window in youth sports as the better athletes see that including the less gifted is more likely to hurt the team's scoring (in the short term) rather than help it. Sportsmanship easily is lessened in the pursuit of victory. Little advantages from missed referee calls, a push here or there, or distracting an opponent with trash talk can help your team win, but at the cost of sportsmanship. While winning is probably more fun than losing, it is not so much fun for a kid who is kept on the bench or never touches the ball or feels like he or she isn't developing much as a player. Finally, and maybe most significantly, your kids won't develop as soccer players or as a team if winning is prioritized.

Let me explain why this is the case. At higher levels, soccer is fundamentally a team game. There is not a clear delineation between offense and defense. Forwards are expected to cover and defend against their opponent's defenders. Defenders are expected to push up to support the offense and even shoot on goal. Roberto Carlos, the great outside defender for Brazil and Real Madrid, scored over 80 goals in his career.

Soccer is like chess and you need superior numbers involved in a play to be effective. Good teams at any level (and all teams at higher levels) aim to "shorten the field"--to get most or all their players in the space of half the field to be compact in defending and to have support for the ball on offense. There is an odd tendency in some youth teams of having defenders hang back near the goal, hands in pockets, waiting for the other team to attack—this is simply bad coaching. It is boring for the defenders, it gives the midfield to your opponents, and it prevents defensive players from being any good whatsoever to your offense. This might sometimes work to stop goals, but more often it just results in a bunch of dispirited defenders and gives your opponents about half the field of free space to run wild. Even if this tactic of holding players back on defense may assure a win, it doesn't develop kids' skills or their understanding of what the game asks at any higher level.

> Coaching Tip: Play games in practice where the only way to score is if everyone on the offensive team is in the offensive half of the field. This teaches kids to push up without any direction from the coach.

So let's leave out winning for a while and see how having the right priorities actually helps develop winners.

Sportsmanship: Winning can be defined many ways. Ultimately, almost none of the kids we work with will be professional athletes. Our kids, we hope, will become productive citizens, good community members, healthy individuals, caring parents, and satisfied in life. For better or worse, there isn't a real scoreboard for these outcomes. All there is the self-awareness, personal motivation, integrity, and responsibility an individual brings to their life. It is not mere wordsmithing to say that kids who develop these values through sports are the real winners. So few will go on to play sports at a higher level, the real priorities of athletics must be character development. Moreover, research has shown that developing these character traits actually maximizes rather than detracts from athletic performance.

Physical Fitness: Sadly, almost 70% of children quit sports by the time they are 13 and only 15% go on to play organized sports after high school. Obviously, the health benefits of physical activity for youth on into adulthood depend on keeping kids active. If we turn them off to sports by middle school, we may never get them back to physical activity.

Fun: To keep kids involved in sports, we need to be sure they are enjoying their experience. Again, an overemphasis on winning can run directly counter to the fun of the game. Drills become mere preparation for games, games become mere quests for victories, losses become failures. Winning undoubtedly is more fun than losing, but surveys show that 75% of children would rather be on a losing team where they get a chance to play than be on a winning team where they are on the bench. Kids want to play!

There are countless ways to make practices and games fun and rewarding, all while helping kids develop as soccer players and a team. Fun and learning are far from mutually exclusive and in fact are self-reinforcing. But emphasizing winning first can easily wring the fun right out of the game, and lead kids right out of the sport.

Teamwork: Sports can instill a sense of what it means to be an athlete and how that translates into what it means to be a part of a team. In the work world, collaborative work has become ever more important—learning how to work in a team is a powerful function of participation in sports regardless of talent. An important part of being a coach is to help players see where their talents fit in, how to value the abilities of others, and how to aim to mesh all this into a whole that is greater than the sum of its parts.

Personal Development: The one final value we hope to promote, maybe above all others, is to help kids feel good about themselves and their participation in sports. This means kids feel they are playing, improving, contributing, and hopefully, that they are capable. There are many ways to help kids feel good—false praise has limited value; real accomplishments and successes hold much more promise. Putting kids in positions that play to their strengths, praising the positive things they do, avoiding shame, making corrections away from the heat of the moment, helping kids and teams continually improve, and making as much as you can fun and full of laughter helps kids build real enjoyment of sports and real self esteem that can form a solid foundation for them as players and people.

The lesson here is simple: Focus on the right priorities— sportsmanship, personal development, teamwork, fitness, fun—and everyone is a winner, not just in spirit, but, you'll find, even in the results on the scoreboard.

The Basics of the Game

In this chapter is the most basic introduction to the game of soccer, introducing terminology and basic skills for those completely new to the game.

Field Names (see labeled drawing)

End line or Goal line: Line across end of the field.

Touchline or Sideline: Lines up and down the side line.

Midfield or halfway line: Line across the center of the field.

Center Circle: 10 yard diameter circle around the center spot that delineates how far defenders have to be away during kickoffs.

Penalty Area/Box: Box where the goalkeeper can use her hands. 18 x 44 yards.

Goal Area/Box: Box in which the ball is placed for goal kicks 6 x 24 yds.

Penalty Spot/Mark: Line 12 yards from the endline where the ball is placed for penalty kicks.

Penalty Arc or "D": Arc at top of the penalty box 10 yards from penalty spot that delineates how far all players must be when a penalty kick is taken. If the offensive team has a player closer than 10 yards, the kick is nullified. If a defender is within 10 yards, the kick can be retaken.

Sounding Like You're from England	
American Word	English Equivalent
Field	Pitch
Cleats	Boots
Uniform	Kit
Game	Match
Schedule	Shedule

Basic Skills

Dribbling: Use any part of the foot. Most players dribble using the inside or top part of the foot to keep the ball in front of herself. The basic idea is to keep the ball in control close to your body and to be able to move with speed (and eventually be able to look up as you do this).

Passing: The basic push pass uses the inside of the foot (the largest, flattest part of the foot). The non-kicking foot is pointed directly at your target and the kicking foot is turned out at a right angle to act like a putter in pushing the ball ahead. Ideally, the player kicking follows through with the knee and foot high, making the ball have some topspin to stay on the ground. Longer passes might use the top of the foot (oddly called the "instep"). Passing with the outside of the foot is a more advanced skill and still has the leg kicking straight forward with the foot pointed toe down and in a little. It is not done by kicking outward from one's hip which generates no power or aim.

Trapping: The idea is to control the ball by slowing the ball down and directing it with part of the body. With passes on the ground, the basic trap is almost opposite the push pass. With the inside of the foot, the player absorbs the ball and aims to direct it in front of him to be dribbled or passed. With balls in the air, the player uses any body part (except hands or arms) to absorb the ball. Inside of the foot, bottom of the foot, thigh, chest, or head can all be used to trap the ball, although practicing most of these skills beyond using feet is usually for more advanced players.

Shooting: You shoot with your instep (top of your foot). This means your toe is pointed down, the support foot is facing your target, and you swing and follow through in the direction you are kicking. Little kids can actually use the top of their foot running straight at the ball since their feet are small. The reason "soccer style" football kickers come at the ball at an angle are 1)they need to angle their foot like this to not stub their toes, and 2) power comes not just from the leg swing but the twisting motion of the upper body—kicking at an angle allows you to better use upper body core strength to help propel the ball. The three principles of shooting are power (the speed of the shot), placement (aiming away from the goalie and usually into corners), and quickness of release (how quickly a player can strike the ball). Keeping your knee over the ball (which also makes you lean more forward than back) helps keep shots low and increases power.

Heading: Heading is not something to push on young players. The usual rule is to teach heading when the kids start trying it out on their own (usually about age 9 or 10). You head a ball with your forehead but the power comes from your stomach muscles. The idea is to have your head in line with your neck as one solid tube that rotates back from the stomach and moves forward to hit the ball forward with the forehead working like a hammerhead. Kids tend to head up through their back and neck and top of their head, like a pogo stick. This is wrong for a lot of reasons (limited power, potential injury, difficult to aim)—have your kids focus on leaning back and snapping forward to practice heading.

Goalkeeping: Goalies can use their hands in the penalty box and act like any other player outside the box. Once a goalie catches or picks up a ball, she has 6 seconds to get the ball back in play by throwing, kicking or rolling it out. Referees tend to be lenient on this time limit, using it just to be sure to prevent intentional delay of game. The goalie can run anywhere in the box with the ball during these 6 seconds. Once the goalie puts the ball down on the ground, she can't pick it up again (but can play it with her feet). Goalies cannot pick up balls intentionally passed back from a teammate but can catch balls headed back by one of her defenders or that come to her if miskicked by a teammate. And goalies can get balls outside the goal box with their feet, dribble it into the box and then pick it up.

Throw-ins: The rule is you must throw the ball in with both feet on the ground, both hands coming over the head with the ball at the same time. This isn't very hard to do right if you don't try to throw the ball far. For kids, this is more a chance to get the ball back into play than some great offensive weapon. Try to encourage kids to get the ball in quickly and legally rather than looking and looking for the perfect opening. The power for throwing the ball comes from arching back to throw and using stomach muscles, not just relying on arm swing.

Chapter 2: Logistics

Looking at youth soccer around the globe, there are all sorts of ways of organizing teams and fields and age groups. While the first priority is to do whatever you can to make sure you have enough kids to play, decisions about logistics should be made in keeping with expertise from experience around the world.

The first thing to note is that in most of the world, there is almost nothing to speak of in terms of organized soccer. Kids in Spain and Brazil and Ghana and Korea learn to play soccer by playing—in the streets and in front of churches, on dirt patches and rocky hillsides, on the beach or in an alley. Kids play soccer, they watch soccer, they talk soccer. This is how they learn the game.

Wherever they play, when kids do have organized soccer, there tend to be strict limits on organized play. In Holland, kids practice two days a week and play one game a week. In Kenya, practice may be held three weekday afternoons, with one game on the weekend. In England, even professional teams tend to play only one game each week, and practice for kids is limited. But these kids also tend to stay after practice to watch older kids and kick around together and play on their own (often incessantly) on non-practice days.

In the US, there has been an enormous surge in organized sports. Particularly since we lack a soccer culture, kids probably need this organization at least to help their developing sense of the game. But we must remember that the aim is not the organization but to have kids be active and love the game and feel good about themselves. Not everything has to be programmed, and even more so, not every free moment of a child's time needs to be scheduled by parents. Remember we are trying to help our kids develop into independent adults who can be self-directed and use their time well. If we as adults determine everything they do with their time, they can't develop the judgment we hope they have as they grow older to use their time well.

Practice and Games
Don't overdo it! Ideally, your organized practices and games leave kids having fun and wishing they could play some more. Despite the

pressure to have kids specialize at age three, scheduling too many days of practice per week can have harmful effects. Specializing narrowly in one sport can lead kids more toward burnout than toward a love of the game. It also limits player development and increases injuries as kids overuse the same muscle groups. The very best athletes—such as Michael Jordan and Wayne Gretzky, grew up playing all sorts of sports. This gave them the coordination and balance and core strength that made them so adaptable and durable and skilled.

More importantly, our hope is to have well-rounded kids with diverse interests. My son likes doing schoolwork and wants to play violin and enjoys reading and needs time to just decompress (in addition to having time for family and friends, to explore outdoors, or for his other athletic interests). There are lots of healthy activities kids should be pursuing in addition to soccer. Give the kids the choice to be dedicated at the level that suits them and their family. The ones who really love soccer and might go on to greatness must have the desire and self-discipline to excel—to train on their own, practice their skills, inspire others to join them to play even when it isn't "official" soccer time.

So at least up to age 12, a maximum of two organized practices and one game per week probably is most appropriate. Remember, an overemphasis on games leads to an overemphasis on winning. As much as kids seem to want to play games, games are an ineffective way to develop soccer ability. First of all, kids get too few touches on the ball in the game (our goalie, for example, may touch the ball only once or twice in a whole game. In one shooting drill, he can easily handle the ball 100 times). Second, no matter how much you want to downplay winning, that is the point of games. You owe it to your kids to at least take the game seriously, so asking your team to work on a weakness like back passing or one touch passing might be a good long term aim that actually hurts your team's chances in the game at hand. Finally, what kids like about games, most of the time, is the winning. Unfortunately, only one team wins, so every game is "useful" (read fun) for one team and not very useful to the other. If you win every time, this is okay for your kids, but it doesn't do much for your opponents—or for the good of the game in your area.

Times

Practices should be from 60-90 minutes. Kids have limited attention spans (if you don't have your own children, you will learn this soon enough!). It is too much work for the coach to keep them entertained and focused for much longer than this. If you can convince your players' parents, the best thing I find is to say we practice for an hour and then if everyone is still having fun when practice is scheduled to end, keep going for a little longer. Usually this results in kids playing on their own after I leave. This is the ideal—you are done with your responsibilities as coach and your kids are self-motivated to keep playing. Less than an hour is usually too short to get anything organized. By time your late arrivals join in and you get some sense of direction, it's time to go. (Plus I hate to have kids spend more time getting to and from practice than the time they are playing.) Chapter 3 details how to organize practice to be active, purposeful, and fun for all.

Team Size

The main aim is to have kids get as many touches on the ball as possible. Soccer is a rather abstract game so seeing where to go with 22 people on the field is almost impossible for young players (especially ones who don't grow up watching the game played on television). Even the best professional teams in the world work on small sided play (3 v 3, 4 v 4) a huge percentage of the time in practice. As I will explain later in more detail, soccer is more easily seen as a game of triangles. Most choices on the field narrow down to 2 or 3 options, not 10. So playing 4 v 4 does more to simulate game situations than 11 v 11 might.

And the fewer the players, the easier it is to see where to go and where not to go (With 11 teammates on the field, it can get very crowded. Even a kid who figures out to move to space away from the ball might run right into a teammate going to the same space). Kids easily grasp that the main idea of soccer is getting the ball, which naturally means being near it. So if there is one ball for 22 players, there will likely be a bunch of kids around the ball. The typical way most coaches counteract this with young kids and large team sizes is by yelling at players to spread out or stay in position. Not very supportive, not very fun for the coach or the player, and not very effective.

14

Much better is simply to play games with fewer players on a smaller field. With 3 or 4 on a side, it is much easier to see where you can go to be open. There are lots of spaces without players and you always have a 1 in 3 or 4 chance of having the ball.

For kids below age 6, you never want to have more than 4 or 5 a side. A field of 30x20 is plenty large for this age and maybe 40x30 for kids slightly more athletic. This isn't a bad team size for all ages (in college, this is almost all we played in practice). If you want to age up a bit towards 11 a side, 7 a side is good for U-8 or even U-10. By middle school (ages 12-13), most teams are playing 11 v. 11, so you may want to build to that with 8, 9, 10 or 11 a side for U-12 (see table below).

Obviously, you don't want to practice in any configuration bigger than the team size in your games. The wasted time and increased frustration by trying to have large sided play at young levels is a huge disservice to everyone involved. In general, you want to scrimmage with the smallest size teams you can organize. The benefits from small-sided games with lots of touches can't be overemphasized.

Field Size

The bigger the field, the more soccer becomes a track meet and the less the kids let the ball do the work. Kids can only run so far, so if you put small kids on an adult size field, there are huge open spaces where kids will just carry the ball with no opposition and no purpose but to plow ahead. Professional soccer players let the ball do the work, passing the ball to open players and working to get superior numbers up in the offensive end of the field. With too much space, kids tend to stop and watch, being so far away from the play once it gets in front of them. And with so much space there is less need to look up and pass. And if no one is going to pass, then no one has to move up to support. All not very good for soccer nor for getting kids involved in the game.

In determining field size for games, remember the soccer sensibility you are trying to develop. You want kids to spread out, use the space, get open, include teammates, support each other, move the ball up and down and back and forth across the field in an effort to stay away from defenders and work towards the goal.

On a too tiny field, this can be very hard, as there is very little space that could be open (which is why high level players practice on very small fields to learn to play under pressure). Too large a field for the number and size of the players, and there is too much space and kids feel out of the play. Field size should correlate with how far a child can run at pace and repeatedly. If your average child can't run from end to end of the field, there is not much chance he or she will keep involved in the play once a game starts.

A professional level field is generally from 100 to 120 yards long and 60-80 yards wide. Scale this down by age, size, stamina and team size and you get something like the following:

Recommended Sizes		
Age Grouping	Team Size	Field Size
U6	5 v 5	30-40 x 20-30
U8	7 v 7	45-70 x 30-50
U10	8 v 8	50-80 x 35-55
U12	11 v 11	70-100 x 50-60

Playing 11 a side on an adult field is unproductive for most players under age 12. Unable to get up and down the field, a few kids hang back on defense near the goal, just waiting for the opponents and a few hang up front never coming back to help on defense. This usually leaves about 60 yards of untended pasture for the midfielders to wear themselves out dribbling the ball unbounded, until reaching the well rested defense. UGLY!

While these field sizes work well for games, for practice, you can do anything. See what happens when you have 3 on 3 on a big field, or 8 v. 8 on a 40 yd field. As we'll discuss in the chapter on practices, different set-ups in practice can all have very different purposes. In games, you can never guarantee what situation a kid will be in—practicing in all different situations helps develop flexibility.

Practice Organization
This is detailed in the next chapter. In short, the idea is to vary what you do and keep it moving. Avoid having kids sit around or wait in

lines or spend time watching. Do things that keep kids active and playing.

It takes time to plan really good practices, and most volunteer coaches/parents are usually not overflowing with free time just waiting to be filled up by practice preparation. (Just reading this book is asking a lot of you, in my opinion.) Rather than having every age group separate and each age group coach using their time to figure out a practice, it can be much more efficient to have one practice for all your kids from age 5-12 and have the plans made by a coach who knows soccer well and is quick in figuring out what drills and activities to use on a given day. The benefits of one practice for all ages are many—less time is spent by each coach planning, younger kids admire the older ones and see a slightly higher level they can aspire to, kids at the higher or lower end of ability in their age group have a chance to be in the middle of a group for a change.

The kids can do most drills together, and when an activity seems unsafe with mixed ages, you can just separate by age group for the time of the activity.

Chapter 3: Running a Practice

Leading practices is your big opportunity both to teach skills and set a tone for your team. There are some great coaching books with hundreds of drills to teach various skills. While having a wide variety of drills in your repertoire can be useful, especially when there is something specific you want to target, for the most part younger kids tend to enjoy a few drills and like predictability, so you can use these over and over again. Moreover, there just isn't that much time for practice, so my problem isn't coming up with enough different drills but trying to fit what I want to do into the time I have for practices.

Some advice about practice scheduling:

1. Up to high school age, 90 minutes is about the maximum time I would aim for in practice, and closer to an hour for kids under about age 8. If kids want to play longer, let them stay and play without the coaches—this is the fun of the game!

2. The maximum number of organized soccer days each week I would say should be 3 (although maybe 4 is okay if you want to follow the American obsession with over programmed youth sports). Ideally, this would be two practices and one game each week, although too many leagues schedule 2 games (or more) per week. For my teams, practices are more fun and inclusive than games, and it is the time kids really can develop skills and strategy, so it is essential to have at least one practice a week if you can. Unfortunately, in our area, we have so many games scheduled that many teams don't have much practice time. Consequently, a lot of coaching is attempted during the games through yelling at kids about where they should go and what they should do. This is ineffective at best and distracting and discouraging too often. It is great if kids want to play more soccer each week—let them get together and play informally (this lets them develop different skills than at organized practice, like fancy dribbling moves a coach may discourage in practice).

3. We practice with all our kids from grades K-6 together. There are several reasons for this. First, it is much more time efficient for the coaches. One coach can plan practice and the other coaches can help out but not have to spend valuable time planning. This works especially well if you have one coach with more significant soccer experience and other coaches who are parents with less experience with soccer. Let the knowledgeable coach plan practices and let the other parent-coaches act as support personnel during practice time. Second, it is good for kids learning the game to have better players as role models. Playing alongside more experienced players allows the beginners to see a bit of what is possible and be part of a higher quality, more controlled game of soccer. Third, kids learn a lot of lessons from being in cross-age groups—older players learn to be sportsmanlike and kind to the younger ones, stronger kids in an age group are challenged by playing up age wise, weaker kids in an age group don't continually feel like they are the weakest players since they will usually be above weaker younger players, the youngest kids are led to be more responsible around older peers, and everyone gets to see each individual has unique qualities to share and kids aren't simply being sorted by level of athletic ability.

4. Although we group all ages together, we do divide up for certain drills and scrimmages, especially when safety is an issue. The method I use for dividing kids is to say "bigger kids over here, smaller ones over there" (or to get really specific, I may say "bigger kids there, middle sized kids there, and smaller ones over here"). The reasoning here is that kids self sort not by age but by level of play. The more athletic and competitive gravitate towards the bigger kids, regardless of age. Older kids wanting less competition or physical play will often join the smaller kids. Kids are quite good at finding their appropriate level of challenge. And interestingly, I find the middle ability kids will switch groups from one time to another—sometimes stretching themselves against the stronger players, sometimes enjoying the chance to be a leader with the younger and less strong players.

Organizing Practice

The most important element of your practices is to set the tone you aim for. For me, the main purpose I aim for is that kids are having fun while developing as soccer players. Thus, I have two primary goals in planning practice—that kids are active and playing with a soccer ball as much as possible and that what they do is fun for them. My basic organization for practice follows the same routine most of the time.

1. Start with unstructured scrimmage: This is the absolutely best way to start practice I have ever seen. As soon a player arrives, you start a game. It may be 1 v 1 at first (you and the first kid). When the next kid comes, make it 2 v 1, the next one makes it 2 v 2...Keep moving the goals back a little and play for fun. When the field gets too crowded (probably about 7 v 7 is the maximum you want at this point to keep everyone having a chance to get the ball), start another game on an adjacent small field (usually I ask bigger kids to move to the new field—they are both more mature about moving and can organize themselves a bit better). This allows you to have kids being active when you and they may be waiting around for stragglers and late-comers. And kids push their parents to get them to practice on time or even early, knowing they get to play as soon as they are there. This immediately sets the tone for practice as fun and active soccer, especially if some of the coaches play and are having fun themselves. This usually lasts about 15 minutes, but if the play is really fun, I may go on for closer to 30 minutes of play.

2. Meeting of the day: This is the one time I talk at the kids, as briefly as possible to convey logistical information, teach the skill of the day, and tell the players about practice goals. I try to have one aim for each practice as this seems to be most effective in helping kids focus their attention. Typically, I go through the skills of dribbling, passing, and shooting the first few weeks, and then choose the skill of the day based on what I see in games. Usually, the next learning goals have to do with field positioning—spreading out, supporting play, switching the field, and defense.

3. Stretching: I often skip this since it is pretty rare that a kid pulls a muscle, so the purpose of stretching is mostly to teach some good lifelong habits and to build a sense of teamwork while everyone is together. Stretching cold muscles (before the blood is flowing) and static stretching (standing around in a circle and leaning one way or another) is generally less effective than dynamic stretching after kids are warmed up a little. If you start with scrimmaging, the kids' muscles will be warm by time you get to stretch. Otherwise, at least some gentle running together (dribbling or passing a ball) or a little soccer drill can be a good warm-up. Dynamic stretching involves stretching while moving—usually with the kids in one or two lines doing the same thing either up 10 yards and jogging back or continually moving around the perimeter of the field (which looks really cool, intimidating, and inspiring). The stretches might include skipping, hopping on one foot, sidestepping, grapevine, knee slaps, buttkicks, high kicks, high jumps, high catches, arm swings, groin openers and closers, lunges, sprints, and anything else that is fun and pushes some part of the body. (See page 56 for a more detailed description.)

4. Drills/Activities: As much as possible, I try to make every skill developing activity as active and involving as possible. With passing or shooting, we may do a brief period of kids in lines hitting a ball back and forth while the coaches give little pointers to individuals. As soon as possible (usually about 5 minutes or so, and often before some kids have mastered the skill), I try to get kids playing a game that requires kids to use this skill. In chapter 5 are some of my favorite activities for particular skills. Almost all the drills have all the kids being active with the ball all the time, and kids learn the skill just through playing the drill, instead of through a lot of direction and explanation from the coach.

5. Scrimmage: For whatever reason, almost every kid wants to scrimmage every practice. Sometimes we don't get to this if we have too many other good things to do, but at the least, I try to get at least 10 minutes of scrimmage at the end of practice. This is a good opportunity to have kids apply whatever skill you are working on that day. It is wise to vary team sizes for scrimmages based on the purpose of practice. If short passing is the goal, small sided scrimmaging makes sense. If you are

working on switching fields, it makes sense to scrimmage on a bigger field with more players. Scrimmaging with different team numbers reinforces the tone of fun and play. Only scrimmaging with the team size you play in official games seems aimed just to prepare kids for game results.

6. Ending Practice: It makes sense to bring closure to practice to review the lessons of the day and to set the stage for your next team event (game or practice). This gives you an organized forum to hand out papers or remind kids about timing for the upcoming games or to make final remarks. That said, it can be hard to get kids' attention at the end of practice. They have just come from a fun scrimmage and are probably now focused on finding their parents and getting home (or are hoping to keep playing). Often, I try to give out any important logistical information at the meeting early in practice and at the end I may just tell kids I am working with that I am done and they are welcome to keep playing without me. This allows you as coach to honor your commitment to the schedule you tell families, but also allows kids who want to keep playing and having fun to enjoy unorganized play with peers. Kids who need to leave can, but others may go on developing their love of the game, leading to better health and better soccer over time.

Notes on Learning Theory: Learning usually involves a cycle of identifying objectives, teaching, and feedback. While sometimes kids will "discover" new insights on their own, in most cases they do better when there is a clear and focused learning objective communicated to the learner, an intervention intended to "teach" towards this objective, and specific feedback to help readjustments and continued improvement.

This needn't involve loads of talking at your players. The learning objective can be communicated quickly, the activity can teach toward the objective through its design (such as restrictions that limit the players to only 3 touches of the ball or giving points for back passes or switching the ball across the field), and feedback can be incorporated as the kids play or with brief remarks afterward.

Keeping the learning objectives secret and hoping kids "figure it out themselves" rarely works, as kids in the US have rarely seen soccer played well and cannot see the objectives they are expected to achieve without explicit modeling or identification by a coach.

Chapter 4: Game Coaching

Practice is the time you really can be active in helping kids develop skills and learn tactics. In soccer, coaches really have limited impact during a game. At the professional level, there are no time-outs, just two forty-five minute halves with a short break at halftime. You are allowed only three substitutes and once a player is replaced, he is done for the game. So there is not a whole lot to do for a coach once a game starts—the game is too fluid and there are limits to what a coach can do to change strategy or make adjustments during a game.

All too often in youth soccer, I see coaches (and parents) screaming the whole game, trying to micromanage the players, cheering every time the ball is booted forward, correcting every time the ball goes the other way. I guess some kids respond okay to this kind of yelling. If nothing else, fear of criticism can make a player try to avoid mistakes. Unfortunately, fear of making mistakes often makes players tight, literally looking over their shoulder rather than focusing on the play in front of them. And, in my experience, fear of making mistakes and fear of losing saps a fair bit of the fun (and skill) out of the game.

I prefer to sit back, cross my legs, and enjoy watching the game from the bench. I try to compliment any good play (for either team) or attempts to make a good play (you catch more bees with honey...). If a player does something unsportsmanlike or mean, they are taken out of the game as soon as possible (sportsmanship being my highest priority). If a player does something I want to correct (which means it is probably both really dumb and a repeated issue), I will wait a few minutes, substitute him out and try to explain the concept to him. Players respond well to this since they know it is rare when I offer this advice (in contrast to shouting coaches who are constantly correcting and admonishing).

The other key to coaching kids is to keep the messages simple and few. Before every game, I write up team goals for the game, usually no more than 3 in total. One is always something on the lines of having fun or enjoying the day. The other one or two are specific tactics I want the team to focus on (see list in box below). I sometimes also make a different sheet specifically for Defenders, Midfielders, and Forwards.

Again, I try to concentrate on 1-3 specific goals for each position, and I even use simple line drawings to reinforce the point for more visual learners. Just before the game, I show the team each of these lists, verbally reviewing the main points I want in their heads when on the field. As the season progresses, I find the kids will just pick up my clipboard if I'm not right there before a game and read the sheets to each other, taking ownership for their direction.

Possible Team Goals (choose 2-3 per game)	
Control the Tempo	Trust
Play with Pace	Teamwork
Pass	Team Speed
Switch Fields	Communication
Marking Defense	Play with Grace and Skill
Contain	Think
Control the Ball	Stay Compact
Backpass	Enjoy!

Substitutes

In youth soccer, coaches have the opportunity to substitute as much as they choose. A big responsibility for the coach is to figure out how to get playing time for all your players. There is much discussion regarding if every player has to play the same amount of time. The key factor here is communication and clarity. Kids can usually tell who are the strongest players and who are the weakest (the in betweens might be harder to discern). And kids know sports are about aiming to win (hopefully without too much pressure about losing). So if you are clear about who plays and why, assuring everyone they will play based on criteria you explain and give everyone a *reasonable* (if not completely equal) opportunity, I think you are okay.

Just to think through this a little: If you play everyone the same amount of time, kids will wonder if you are really putting out the best team to be competitive (why would you keep your best players on the bench if you are losing?). If you play only the stronger players, it seems all you care about is winning and this discourages everyone else.

Since I often have kids on my team who may be as much as 4 years apart, I tend to show respect for the older ones by giving them slightly more playing time and the honor of starting the game (although I love having the younger ones get a chance to play some against older competition). I try to have equal time for most players (usually about 10-12 out of my 17 person team). But I will keep a few players in the game somewhat more if I think they can help keep the team organized and anchored so the rest of the team can play its best (I don't think the kids gain much from having more playing time but with a team so disorganized or inept that it is just kickball. I'd rather have a bit of inequality so that everyone enjoys quality time when they are playing).

The one time I will be least sensitive to equalizing playing time is in tournaments. This is for two reasons—tournaments seem a time to put your best foot forward and test yourselves against a lot of other teams with the aim of winning a trophy. All kids on a team take pride in this ultimate triumph, whether or not everyone plays the exact same time (although if a kid doesn't play at all this can be terribly discouraging). More importantly, most tournaments involve some kind of qualifying for a final round of additional games. If you lose the early games, there are no additional games. It seems better to have somewhat less equal playing time in a qualifying game with the chance to play more time in more games overall than to have equal playing time, losing early and going home. The reward for winning is more playing! That is the only reward most kids need.

When to substitute is another coaching decision. Subbing too frequently can disrupt the flow of the team. Putting in a whole big group at once can totally alter the tenor (for good or ill). I tend to substitute during the game rather than at breaks to make it simpler for me. I can then talk to the team as a whole at breaks without sorting out who is playing where. Then I may quickly put in subs when the next half starts once I see where my players are lined up. My goal in substituting is to retain the team flow and level of play, and so usually I substitute one player at a time so each one can fit in as the players change.

On Rewards and Celebrating
This is mostly a factor of your personality. I am not a brownies and pizza rewards coach. In fact, I am not even a cookies and snacks-in-practice coach☺. I barely remember to stop for kids to drink water! (Not a great thing to miss actually.) From my view, the reward of soccer is playing soccer. I love the game and to me this is the best thing

we can do. Stopping for water or snacks or breaks, to me, is just less time to play (obviously not all kids see this the same way, but it is infectious for them to see this enthusiasm).

How you celebrate wins as coach is up to you. Expressing true joy is great for kids to see. If you really are excited by a game, show it. But if you don't think winning the Podunk Village U-6½ year old Tournament is the biggest thing in your life, a low-key reaction is fine too. The kids are likely to get innately excited about winning—you don't have to do this for them. And losing is disappointing whether you show displeasure or not. Personally, I tend to react with little excitement win or lose. The emotion I try to convey is pride in my team achieving the goals I list before a game—playing their best, having fun, working on a skill or tactic (or expressing some small level of disappointment if these goals are not met). I let the kids react to the score of the game—they are perfectly capable about getting excited about wins, and are saddened by losses—seeing their coach remain even through all this helps them see that life goes on regardless.

Most kids love cookies or brownies or pizza after practice and this social time eating together can be as bonding as any team time playing soccer. Just try not to tie these treats to some quid pro quo about game results or behavior or some other meritorious ideal you are trying to reach. The rewards of winning are the satisfaction of winning. Special treats for winning starts to feel like pay for play. (Win and you get pizza; lose you get nothing). Let the intrinsic motivation of doing your best, supporting your teammates and working together be the inspiration. External rewards tend to lower internal motivation, and in the long run reduce kid's athletic participation unless these rewards are there.

The other reason I don't do a lot with food rewards is my emphasis on learning responsibility outweighs my emphasis on winning. I want the kids I work with to begin to take responsibility for themselves, so I expect them to bring their own water and food. If I provide that for them, they become dependent on me rather than developing the independence we hope for them as they mature. For day-long events, I still bring extra food and water for kids who forget, but the natural consequences of going thirsty or hungry for a 1 hour practice or game can be a great lesson in teaching a child to be more self-responsible. Of course, for kids who cannot afford food, helping them out is more than appropriate, and if health is hurt in any significant way by poor nutrition, it is your responsibility to look out for the well being of each of your players.

I am not a fan of individual awards in games, tournaments, or end of season ceremonies. Soccer is a team game and at the highest levels it takes all 11 players on the field for a team to be successful. Even a player who never touches the ball in the game helps by creating open space for others or closing down where opponents can play. And even players who don't play in a game are part of the quality of a team by what they contribute in practice in helping others develop. So recognizing individual players doesn't make a lot of sense at any level in soccer. And for younger players, individual honors can exacerbate the negative aspects of competition, limiting success to not just one winning team, but to one person, at the cost of leaving everyone else out as "losers." Much better are team awards for spirit of the game (an idea taken from ultimate Frisbee where the trophy for the most fair minded and good spirited team is equal in size and prestige to the tournament champion) or best teamwork (the highest honor for my team was not just winning their first tournament, but being the first team ever awarded the Most Valuable Player trophy instead of being it given to a player). And for end of season awards, I always try to give the same, hopefully useful, award to each player, recognizing each for doing their best. We give our kids soccer balls at the end of the year rather than trophies—they can cost little more than trophies, encourage kids to play on their own, and can serve as nice mementos if you bring Sharpie markers so teammates can autograph the ball.

Pre-Game/Post-Game

Again, remember your aims—fun, responsibility, teamwork, sportsmanship. Before the game, I have only two purposes: 1) Make sure the players are physically warmed up to play, 2) Try to get the team mentally focused on the goals for the game. For physical warm-ups, dynamic stretching is preferable to static stretching (see warm-up drills, page 56). This not only is better for generating blood flow and loosening muscles, it can be psychologically bonding for your team and intimidating to your opponents (and it is what pro teams do). Once the kids are warmed up, I meet with the kids just before the game to review the goals and the line-up. That's it. The focus is being ready to play and letting the kids at it. It is their game, not mine, so I try to minimize the time with me and let them get to the play at hand.

Post game, it is hard to get much attention from kids. Again, I have only two aims: 1) Team unity and 2) Sportsmanship. I get the kids together and if I'm lucky, I can get about 30 words of their attention. I tell them a couple things they did well, maybe one thing we need to work on and then send them off to show their sportsmanship, thanking the refs (a soccer tradition where at least the captain shakes hands with the referee (no matter how lousy a job he or she may have done☺) and then shaking hands and thanking the opponents. I am on a crusade to eliminate the perfunctory "Goodgame, goodgame" handslap lineup. This feels completely insincere to me and close to rude. Instead, I emphasize the long held soccer tradition of showing respect and appreciation for the opposition by looking each player in the eye, shaking hands, and offering some specific complimentary words (nice defending, good shot on goal, you made me work for the ball…). At the highest levels, as my son points out, players exchange jerseys with an opponent they valued; the least we can do with kids is ask them to at least really shake hands and say thanks for giving us a chance to play the game.

Sportsmanship Note: Everyone seems to know that in youth sports you line up to shake hands after the game. Try to teach your kids to thank the other team on their own volition when the game ends and while still on the field. It feels forced to get your team together and direct them to line up and shake hands (or slap hands) with the other team lined up by their coach. It is a tradition in soccer to shake hands with your opponents on the field. I find the players talk much more with their opponents and are more appreciative when this gesture is done naturally before the teams meet with coaches and need to be directed to line up. Plus, it is much better for coaching to not have to rush your remarks to your players so they can go line up to shake hands. Do the congrats and thanks as the players leave the field, then you can meet with your team to debrief as long as you need.

Teaching from the Bench

The most productive thing you can do during the game is teach a bit to those on the bench. Of course, your most important teaching is modeling good sportsmanship and spirit. But as you watch the game, you can point out tips and insights to players on the bench. Since kids may not be most focused on listening when watching a game, you often have more impact if you invite a kid to sit next to you for specific pointers. General commentary to everyone (or no one in particular) may get picked up on by alert kids or may not be heard. I know some of my players love listening to my general commentary on the game (I try to make it all positive, or at least good humored), but others only hear anything if I address them personally. If you have specific lessons to teach, be sure to address this directly to a player.

When players come out of the game for substitutes, you have the opportunity to educate while checking in with players. Some kids are very hard on themselves, never being satisfied with their level of play. Other kids are very verbally critical of teammates. Gentle and clear support and encouragement can redirect some of these negative sentiments.

Time Management

Soccer is a game of flow and tempo. Alert coaches (and players) can feel the momentum in a game. When things are working against you, you want to change the tempo. This usually means slowing things down and breaking the opponents' momentum. There are a few tricks to working the clock in soccer. The easiest is to milk any stopped ball—goal kicks, throw-ins, free kicks, even when the goalie has the ball. If things aren't going your way, try to have your players slow things down and give your team a chance to take a breath. Conversely, if your team is on the move, get the ball in play fast before your opponents can regroup.

The other great skill is how you use subs. Subbing can be really disruptive (both good and bad). It often takes time for a team to settle into a tempo. Putting in a sub early in the game can muck things up just when things may begin to gel. Putting in a whole big group of subs at once at any point in the game tends to really mess things up. If your team is playing horribly, big subbing can disrupt the struggles. But if your kids are doing okay, judicious subbing and putting in players one at a time is advisable. Late in the game, if you are leading, subbing one player at each stopped ball (especially for a player on the far side of the field) can take some time off the clock and disrupt the flow of the opposing team. You shouldn't take advantage of this to the point of being unsportsmanlike, but it is a rule abiding strategy to help your kids weather fatigue and pressure late in the game.

Tactics

This is the area where a coach has the most potential influence on the results of a game. While you shouldn't try to micromanage your players during a game, you can set up a strategy that gives your kids the best chance of finding success on the field. Experience with soccer can really help with tactics, but a lot can be learned with reading, watching high level soccer, and a lot of common sense.

Line-ups: Line-ups are listed from the defense forward (no one mentions the goalie since this is assumed to be the one furthest back), so a common professional line-up is 4-3-3 (four defenders, three midfielders, three forwards). The other common professional lineup is 4-4-2, and once in a while you see a 5-3-2 or 4-5-1. Looking at these numbers, you may quickly notice the emphasis on greater numbers of defenders. Although this is partly because defense matters (if you are never scored on, you cannot lose), this doesn't necessarily mean these are defensive formations. In fact, when my men's team played a 5-3-2, this was our most offensive line-up.

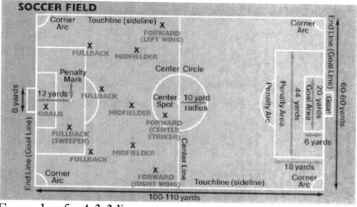

Example of a 4-3-3 line-up

To understand why this is so, you have to remember that soccer is a game of flow. There aren't just defenders who hang out to protect their own goal and forwards who wait up front to take shots. Players are expected to play the whole length of the field—the Dutch team coined the term "Total Football" for this approach used by every team worldwide. When their team has possession, defenders push up on to support their offense (and some defenders are great goal scorers). On defense, forwards are expected to come back and cover the opponent's defenders and midfielders.

This really comes down to a simple numbers game—if you can get all your players up on offense, you have 10 of your team versus how ever many defenders the other team gets back. My 5th-6th grade championship teams basically always outnumber their opponents on both ends of the field. With other coaches telling their 3 or 4 defenders to stay back and their 3 or 4 forwards to stay up, we are playing 10 on 6 on offense and have 9 or 10 defenders against their 6 or 7 offense players when they have the ball.

For my men's team, the 5-3-2 was offensive because it freed defenders to go up almost at will, knowing that if 2 defenders went forward, there were still 3 back to defend if the ball was lost. Besides being advantageous to have numbers on both ends of the field, it is a heck of a lot more fun for your players to be part of the game on both ends of the field. Standing back on defense all game waiting for the ball to come at you just to kick it away can get pretty boring (as evidenced by kids who keep their hands in their pockets on defense or chat with their peers). Moving forward gets defenders into the game, and "shortens" the field so your team makes it harder for the opponents to find open space. Typically, this means keeping your team shape in about ½ the length of the field: when your team has the ball near the opponent's goal, your defenders are at about midfield (including when the opponents have a goal kick). If a defender gets beat around midfield, there is a very good chance she can chase the opponent down on the long run to goal (if the opponent actually can dribble half the length of the field, shoot on goal, and score before one of your players can catch him, tell your players to shake the scorer's hand in admiration—it just doesn't happen that much).

Positions:

Forwards—The primary job of forwards is to score goals. At the youth level, this usually happens one of three ways. 1) Some gifted or lucky kid dribbles by some defenders and dribbles almost all the way into the goal. 2) The ball bounces around off a bunch of players and someone knocks it in from close range. 3) The offense plays the ball across the field from one side (where all the defenders tend to congregate) to the "weak" side where there are few defenders and some open forward has all the time in the world to put the ball in the goal. Nothing against the first two, but these involve less team play and are less like more advanced soccer than the third way. As tempting as it is to have the "best" player dribble past weaker opponents and score, this develops lousy habits both for the strong player, who never develops field sense or vision or passing, and everyone else, who learn to stand around watching, knowing they won't ever get the ball back. And at some point in his career, your "best" player will face defenders who can shut him down, and he'll lack the skills to use his teammates.

The skills you want your forwards to learn are to control the ball, hold the ball and drop the ball to teammates, and to play the ball at angles—passing across the field or between defenders. This penetrates the defense and creates the openings where goals come from.

The other skill for forwards is to shoot quickly, with power and placement. This is obviously easier said than done. The best goal scorers in the world have a very quick release. This is advantageous in beating defenders and surprising goalies before they are ready. Power is obviously important but placement can be even more crucial. Not even the best goalies can save most shots that are low and in the corners. Unfortunately, many young players look at the goalie when shooting, and that is where the ball tends to go. Try to get them to look at where they want to shoot (corners)—it works.

Midfielders—You want Midfielders who can run—a lot. Expected to be up front on offense and back on defense, this position gives shape to your team. If the outside midfielders stay wide, and the center midfielder distributes the ball in all directions, the rest of the team will probably be more or less in the right places. You want midfielders who have good judgment, knowing when to pass, when to hold the ball, when to challenge for the ball and when to contain and drop back. You hope to teach your midfielders to read the game to decide how to control the middle of the field—having a sense when to slow down or speed up play, when to help the ball switch direction, when to try to create open spaces on offense or close spaces down on defense.

Defenders—Too often coaches put the worst athletes on defense and this is a huge mistake. Because of the importance of preventing goals, you want as skillful defenders as you can find. Especially if you want your defenders to help out on offense, you want good athletes in the back.

The other mistake with defenders is their initial belief they are supposed to always steal the ball from the opponents. The job of the defender, it should be emphasized, is *to prevent the other team from scoring*. More important than getting the ball, this means preventing the other team from shooting on goal. The first priority for a defender is to **contain** the opposing player, forcing the ball away from the goal—outside and back. The defender needs to stay between the offensive player and the goal—this is the key to defense, not stealing the ball. When a defender steps in to steal the ball, the offensive player may get past him and then the offensive player is in on goal unheeded.

Likewise, when a defender has the ball, she wants to play it out wide as much as possible. Balls played through the middle can be dangerously stolen in front of the goal. Confident teams, however, may pass the ball among central defenders, especially if they aren't under pressure.

Finally, defenders have to be taught to push up when their team has the ball. So focused on preventing scoring, the natural tendency is to stay back protecting the goal. The best way to protect the goal is to stop the ball well away from the goal, and this happens when the team is pushed forward and remains compact, limiting the space available to the opposition.

Where to Put Players: Some coaches prefer to have players try out different positions all the time. This makes sense if some positions are less desirable, which is true only if you don't play full field soccer. If you play total soccer, defenders probably have as much fun as forwards, and may even score as often. My main consideration in choosing positions is to place players where they will feel most successful. Especially for younger players learning the game, it is hard enough to learn one position, let alone several. I try to discover each player's individual strengths and then find the position that plays to these strengths. Keeping players in their strongest position allows them to develop throughout the season and to feel a level of success less likely if they change positions often. (Of course, if our team is winning by a lot, I move players to new positions to keep the score down and so our players can have fun trying out other positions).

The box below outlines some of the qualities I consider to assign positions based on individual strengths:

Qualities for Positioning Players	
Fearless, cool, unfazed, fun, maybe a little wacky	Goalkeeper
Competitive, fast, hates to lose, tough, verbal, likes to head the ball	Central Defender
Good judgment, coordinated, calm, fit, good vision	Central Midfield
Competitive, fast, quick, creative, fun, can use both feet, likes to head the ball	Forward
Reliable, smart, good judgment (even if not terribly fast, skilled, or tough)	Outside defender
Good runner, fit, fast	Outside midfield

Set Plays: At higher levels, something like 60% of goals are scored on set plays (when the ball is stopped for a violation or stoppage in play). At younger levels, these restarts are less about scoring than getting the ball back in play, learning some soccer "tricks" and hopefully not to give away the ball in a place that lets the other team have a chance on goal.

Kickoffs: The wrong way to kick off (which is surprisingly popular with kids) is to kick the ball downfield. This violates rule #1 of sports—don't give the ball away to the other team. Think about it—you have

11 kids on one side of the field and they have 11 on the other. You kick the ball downfield where they have 11 and you have none?

The ball has to roll forward at first on a kickoff, but then it should be passed back to your own players. This will bring the opposing team players forward and you can move some of your players into the offensive end. Then when the ball does go forward, you have more equal numbers. This also reminds your players that it is okay to pass back, and that soccer is a full field game, not just a mono-directional march towards the goal.

Throw-ins: When the ball goes over the sideline, a throw-in is awarded to the opposing team from the one who touched it last. Although kids treat throw-ins as the one time they really think about where they mean to pass the ball, it should be treated as just a way to get the ball back in play, hopefully in the possession of your team.

What usually is ineffective is having a player take the ball to the touchline, searching and searching for an open player. If the other team knows how to cover, it is unlikely anyone will get open. If this is the case, encourage your players to throw the ball down the sideline. This often results in the other team knocking the ball out of bounds and in this way, the ball advances downfield.

More effective is picking the ball up quickly and getting it back in play before the other team is set up defensively. A big trick is to throw the ball in well before reaching the touchline. There is no rule saying you have to be near the sideline for throw-ins, as long as the ball lands in bounds. Throwing in from several feet away from the sideline usually totally fools opponents who figure you will walk to the line before throwing the ball back in.

Defending on throw-ins involves covering players one on one, goal side (defenders should always be between the player they cover and the goal the opponents are heading for). For some reason, youth defenders often stand between their opponent and the ball, which usually just results in the ball going over their head and letting the offensive kid have the ball without a defender between her and the goal.

Goal Kicks: In youth soccer, this is, somewhat paradoxically, about the most dangerous play for the team with the ball. Little kids can barely get the ball out of the penalty box, so it often ends up just barely leaving the box right in front of the goal to be scooped up by an offensive player who is 18 yards from goal with nothing between him and the goal but the solitary goalkeeper.

It is important to understand the rules on goal kicks. There are 4 key conditions:

1) The kicking team can have as many players in the penalty box as they wish.
2) The ball has to leave the penalty box before it is touched by any player to be in play.
3) If the ball is touched before leaving the box, there is a re-kick.
4) The opposing team has to have all its players out of the box.

Typically in youth soccer, all the defenders leave the box, the opposing team lines its forwards at the top of the box, and the ball is kicked just out of the box where a forward from the opposing team gets the ball and is in on goal. While it can be hard to totally avoid this, there are a few concepts to emphasize:

1) Try to have the person taking the kick aim the ball wide, even out of bounds is better than up the middle.
2) Keep some of your defenders in the goal box. Then, if an opposing forward gets the ball, there is at least someone besides the goalie to slow down their run at the goal.
3) If the kick is going to barely get out of the box or go to an opposing player, teach one of your players to touch the ball before it leaves the box, thereby resulting in a chance to take the kick again.

With younger kids, you may choose to have teams take goal kicks from the 18 yard line, with the defensive team at least 10 yards away or even past the halfway line. This makes these goal kicks less tense and more like "real" soccer where this is really a chance for the team taking the kick to begin their offensive play.

Free kicks: There are two types of free kicks that occur after fouls: Direct and indirect. Direct means you can shoot right at the goal, while indirect means someone has to touch the ball before it can go in the goal. It used to be the case that on indirect kicks the ball had to roll one full revolution before being touched by another player. Since that rule has changed to only requiring the ball is touched in any way by a teammate, indirect kicks can quickly become direct if one player just holds her foot over the ball and taps it before a teammate shoots on goal.

Corner kicks are direct, as are penalty kicks and basically any violation that is considered mean to an opponent or the spirit of the game (pushing, tripping, handling the ball). Less offending fouls such as dangerous play or obstruction are indirect. In either case, with youth soccer there are only a few basic plays on free kicks.

If the ball is within shooting range of the goal, the best plan is to shoot on goal and have your other players run at the goal for any rebounds or deflections. If the ball is outside shooting range, the choices are two:

1) Kick long and across the field hoping to get the ball to a player who can attack the goal (the reason to kick across is that balls played at angles are harder to defend as the ball goes across the defense and can be received by different players if it is missed by the first one or two or three. Also, balls hit straight up the field often just slip by your player and go directly to a waiting defender or the goalie or out of bounds).

2) Play the ball short to a teammate to get the ball back into play. This can be especially effective if your team plays the ball quickly. Most opposing teams expect you to kick long and take the time to move your players forward. While the opponents are all backpedaling and waiting for you to set up, your player just plays it to an open teammate close by and you are back off to the races! This latter tactic is what professional teams use most of the time, unless they can hit a ball into the goal box from the free kick in the hopes of getting a shot on goal.

Defensively, players must be 10 yards away from a stopped ball on free kicks. If the ball is within shooting range, the defensive players should form a "wall" of 2-5 players who stand squeezed together blocking one side of the goal (with the goalie covering the other side). The other defenders should cover the offensively most dangerous players (those closest to the goal).

Defensive Tactics. (This repeats information above but is so important it bears repetition.) The basic idea of defending is to prevent the other team from scoring. Your initial inclination to this may be to assign a group of players to stand in front of the goal to keep the ball from scoring. There are all sorts of reasons this is a bad idea, not the least of which is that it is boring for your defenders and leaves them out of the rest of the game. Thought about differently, you may realize that you could also prevent the other team from scoring by keeping them as far away from your goal as possible. If they never get the ball in your side of the field, they aren't very likely to score!

While your team probably can't keep the ball in the opponent's end all game, they can "shorten" the field by keeping compact lengthwise in a 40 or 50 yard area. The rules of soccer promote this by not allowing offensive players to be behind all the defenders without the ball (this is called being offside, explained further in the chapter on rules). Because of the offside rule, leaving your defenders back allows opponent's offensive players to hang out near your goal. If your defenders push up, the opponent's players have to drop back, to remain onside and to cover all your players. And if your team is compact, they limit the open space for the opponents to have the ball.

Most soccer defense is "man-to-man" (called "marking up" in soccer). The basic idea is to have the most dangerous offensive players "marked up" (covered) by a defensive player. The most dangerous offensive players are usually those closest to the goal (in the center of the field and nearest the goal line). You hope to teach your defenders to mark up, staying between the offensive player and the goal. Defenders should learn to not necessarily always try to steal the ball, simply working to keep the ball away from the goal (forcing the play outside and back as much as possible). Most teams use a "sweeper" as the last defender who isn't expected to mark a player but is free to sweep up behind everyone else if the ball gets behind the other defenders.

Young defensive players seem to think their job is to steal the ball. In soccer, the real job of the defender is mostly to delay their opponent and channel them away from the goal, where they either lose the ball through a mistake or pass it. Balls may get stolen from bad passes, but it is rare a defender takes a ball away from a player dribbling (pro players are just too good and fast to take the ball from). The risk of lunging to steal the ball from a player and missing can be high—the offensive player is suddenly undefended and free to go to the goal. The safe, smart play is to teach defenders to "contain" their opponent (back away and force the player away from the goal, being sure the offensive player doesn't get past you).

The other point to emphasize with defenders is the adage, "When in doubt, kick it out." No one scores when the ball is out of bounds and giving away a throw-in slows the play down and lets your defenders get back to reorganize. Kicking the ball wide keeps the ball away from the goal; kicking it out really slows things down.

Making it Fun

Making it fun is the key to it all. If kids (and families) are enjoying soccer, they will be more committed and involved and as a result, the kids will become better players (and probably win more games). There are many ways to make it fun, the most basic of which is to make sure it is fun for you as a coach. Here are some of the ways I make soccer fun for me and my team.

1. Playing with the kids: I like to play as much as I can with the kids in scrimmages. First of all, I just enjoy playing soccer, so if I can play, I am happier (plus I can usually look good against most kids☺). More importantly, I can help make the game more controlled, model smarter play, show kids what is possible with better play, and help kids work on tactics I identify (for example pushing the ball wide to keep players from bunching or making sure to switch sides with the ball). I sometimes join in drills too, but usually these take more of my

attention to organize and teach and evaluate than scrimmages where I can coach while I play. It is important to be fair if adults play, so one team doesn't feel disadvantaged by not having an adult. I usually join the weaker players to make things more even and to help these kids elevate their game a bit.

2. <u>Family Soccer</u>: Like when I play with the kids, having parents play helps model more controlled and sportsmanlike play. Our Family Soccer Saturdays have become the high point of my week. Not only is this good for the kids' soccer play, but it is great for families. Kids and parents are sharing quality, healthy time, kids see their parents learning something new, parents can show kids that the results of the game are less important than the game itself, and everyone has fun. I can't recommend this highly enough. A small caveat: you may have to pull a few parents aside to help them bring their intensity and competitiveness to an appropriate level for the spirit of safe and fun family soccer.

3. <u>Play-by-Play Commentary</u>: Always good for smiles—I guess it makes kids feel like they are on TV or something, but a little commentary during scrimmages and games seems to amuse the kids (especially those on the bench). It also allows you to point out lessons to your players sometimes without needing to be directive. Slipped into the play-by-play, a little comment about "The Eagles seem to be struggling to spread the field today" can get your point across without making the players feel criticized. One of my players says she likes being on the bench more than playing because she likes hearing the comments.

4. <u>Celebrating Goals</u>: In most of the world, goal scoring is cause for euphoric celebrations—shirts pulled over the head, dances, flips, hugs and kisses, fireworks, horn blaring, music playing.... A big part of this is that soccer is not a high scoring game, so when a goal is scored, it is worth celebrating. Kids like to emulate these celebrations—teaching them a few of these crazy reactions to goals always leads to smiles and teaches kids that the purpose of the game is scoring and enjoying when this happens. Check out Youtube to see some good models of goal celebrations.

5. <u>Keep it moving</u>: Kids have more fun when they are participating. Standing in lines, watching others play, and waiting around all are less fun than playing. I move quickly

41

from one activity to another—maybe 10 minutes maximum for each activity and then on to the next one. Especially if you use drills repeatedly, the amount of time for direction giving can be minimized, and the time to be active maximized.

6. <u>Loose Rules and Boundaries</u>: Originally, soccer was played with no boundaries at all. Games ran over hill and dale wherever the ball went. Younger players can get really fixated on rules and "fairness," sometimes more than they attend to the enjoyment of playing. I knew I had made great progress with my players when they got comfortable playing loose with the rules in pick-up games. You just get more playing in if the game doesn't stop when the ball is a few inches outside a line or it glances off a player's hand. It isn't that you want kids to ignore the rules, but it is great when they see that who gets what throw-in or what foul is called is a lot less important than playing and having fun regardless of the result. You can model this when you are playing with the kids, like once in a while picking up the ball and throwing it in the goal and smiling. The kids will all gang up on you and the goal doesn't count, but they all get a good laugh out of this.

Connect Games to Practice: Keep your goals forefront for both games and practice—the focal point for practice should come from what you see in games. What you stress in games should be something you have worked on in practice. It is best to focus on only a very limited number of ideas at any one time with youth players. Generally, I have one or two main learning goals for practice and about the same for a game. For example, in practice, we may work on the technique of passing and the tactic of switching fields with passes. In the ensuing game, I will emphasize switching fields, and maybe add an idea about defending as what I want my teams to focus on.

Referees and Rules of the Game

Referees for youth soccer in the US are not always up to the quality you or the players might wish. Mostly, you have to just accept this, although having a good familiarity with the rules yourself can help educate referees (especially if done before or after the game, rather than when you disagree with a call). A great way to develop officiating talent and to lessen the tendency to have parents or players shouting at refs is to have kids officiate. This has several benefits:

1. It helps the kids reffing learn the rules of the game and learn to empathize with the difficulty of reffing.

2. It discourages adults from yelling at the ref since this means yelling at children.

3. It gives a role to kids who may not be as competitive or may be less athletic.

4. It is much more likely that any of your kids will have a future in sports as a paid referee than as a paid player. This can be a great way to keep involved in sports, and at the highest level, it is well paid and well respected.

It is great to give kids practice with this aspect of sports. And if you use a 3 ref system, as is used at the higher levels everywhere in the world, you can use an experienced adult referee as the head field official and the kids can learn the ropes as linesmen who signal out of bounds and offsides. This maximizes the precious resource of qualified refs while developing officiating skill among youth.

The rules of soccer are relatively few and simple. When I was a kid, there were supposedly only 17 rules, although these have been expanded over time to try to clarify things. Most of the obscure rules don't arise in the course of a season, so I will focus on ones you benefit from knowing as a coach.

1) "Mean" actions are fouls. Kicking someone, tripping, pushing, etc. are not permitted. If done with some degree of intention or malice, they may result in a yellow card (a warning) or a red card (ejection from the game).
2) Dangerous plays are really important to enforce for younger kids. When a player is on the ground anywhere near the ball, it is important to stop play to avoid injury. Likewise, high kicks (above waist height) or kids putting their head down near waist

height are also dangerous. Really enforce these for the safety of all.

3) Throw-ins require the player throwing the ball to have both feet on the ground and throw with both hands over the head. This is surprisingly hard for young kids—try to think of this as a way of getting the ball back in play rather than some way of making a great pass. The quicker the ball is back on the field, the less likely the thrower will be tempted to try to throw hard or far and make an illegal throw-in. Of course, all that happens if the throw is illegal is the other team gets to throw it in. Your team will get the ball back soon enough.

4) There is no fouling out in soccer. Thus, fouls are not really a big deal although young kids act like they made some huge mistake when whistled for a violation. When I played in college as a defender, I sometimes racked up the fouls against super fast players. I didn't try to foul them, but fouling them was a lot better than letting them run right past me. It is unsportsmanlike to try to foul opponents, but it is okay to teach kids that fouls are not the end of the world, and are just stoppages of play when a rule is broken.

5) Hitting the ball with your hand is not necessarily a violation all the time. The ruling depends on the ball being hit by the hand with intent or to the player's advantage. So a ball shot at a kid that hits his hand that is already in front of his chest probably isn't a hand ball. But a ball that a kid reaches up to grab or one that hits an extended hand and drops to that player's feet is probably a foul. Again, no big deal, just a restart kick for the opposition (unless in the penalty box where it results in a penalty kick and an almost certain goal).

6) Offsides is probably the most confusing rule for players and coaches. It isn't that complicated in reality once you understand it. The rule states the player is offsides if when the ball is passed, she has less than two opposing players between her and the goal. But to be called offside, the ball has to be played to the player in the offside position. If someone is in an offside position but the ball is not passed towards him (or if a teammate just dribbles the ball in on goal himself), offside should not be called.

If you have the ball, you can never be offside (my most talented forward thought he had to keep two players between him and the goal even when he had the ball, thereby limiting his scoring until he figured this out). On corner kicks, because the ball is on the endline, you cannot be offside. Also you cannot be offsides on throw-ins because the rules say so, and you cannot be offside if you are out of bounds (so you will see smart players step over the endline after passing the ball across from the endline so as not to be offside). If the offensive player is even with the last defender when the ball is passed, that is considered onside. Again, kids think being offside is horrible, but it just means the opponents get the ball. Some of the best scorers in the world (like Thierry Henry of France or Didier Drogba of Ivory Coast) consistently get as close to offsides as they can. They get called offsides a lot but if they get through once or twice a game, that is almost a sure breakaway goal.

Defensively, many teams try to use an "offsides trap." This involves pushing defenders forward trying to "trap" the offensive players behind the defense and therefore offsides. Unfortunately, sometimes the referees miss this call, and then the defenders have a footrace to try to catch the offensive player out ahead. The advantage of pushing all your players forward to make the offense offside is that it forces the offense further from the goal. Even if the ball is played over the defense, it is a long run for the offensive players and usually a fast defender can catch up to them.

The red team defenders are pushing up towards midfield to catch the two white jersey players in an offside position.

7) Free kicks can be taken as soon as the ball is stopped. The kicking team has the right to ask for all defensive players to be 10 yards from the ball, and then they have to wait for the referee to signal the restart. But if the team with the ball wants to play it quickly, they can just set the ball in place and kick. This can really confuse youth teams whose defense is slow to get organized.

8) The goalkeeper must be protected. Goalkeeping can be a dangerous position and players need to respect the goalie's health. If the goalie's hand is on the ball, it is ruled as in his control. Teach your players not to try to kick the ball out of the goalie's hands—although it seems this is competing to score, it can result in a bad injury to the goalie (such as getting kicked in the head) and no score is ever worth this kind of injury in youth soccer.

9) Out of bounds: The whole ball has to be over the whole line to be out of bounds. Most American sports rule that just touching the line is out—this is not the case in soccer so teach your players to keep playing until the whistle blows.

10) Advantage Rule: The referee is instructed not to stop play for a foul if it is to the advantage of the fouled team to keep playing. So even if your player is fouled but the ball remains in your team's possession, the referee might not call a foul or will call it a bit late after it is clear your team has lost the ball. Teach patience with this.

11) In "real" soccer around the world, the referee has full discretion over almost everything, especially the clock. Unlike American sports such as football and basketball that end "at the buzzer," refs are never supposed to stop a soccer game until the ball is in a "neutral space." This means an offensive play shouldn't be stopped regardless of what the clock says. Sadly, this tradition is not followed much in the US but it is worth talking to refs about this.

12) Finally, referees are the highest authority in the game. In international matches, the flag of the referee is raised higher than both the opposing teams. Despite the uneven quality of referees, it is good to teach your players to respect the refs. One tradition to follow is to have players shake hands with the refs after the game, a sportsmanlike gesture to end the game.

Chapter 5: DRILLS

Dribbling

Sharks and Minnows: Speed Dribbling. All players have a ball and line along one end line—these are the minnows. 1-3 players without the ball are in the middle of a 30-40 yard field as Sharks. After calling, "Minnows, minnows come over," all the minnows try to get to the other end of the field without having their ball kicked out of the boundaries by a shark. If their ball is kicked out, they immediately become a shark and can attack other minnows. Keep going back and forth until there are no more minnows. The last couple minnows can be the sharks to start the next round.

Knockout: Teaches shielding the ball, and keeping your head up. Everyone has a ball and is dribbling in a confined space (maybe 20 x 20 yard box for 20 players). Players try to kick the ball away from others and out of bounds while not losing their ball. Once your ball is kicked out, you leave the square until the next game begins.

Monsters: Like Knockout but 1-3 "Monsters" don't have a ball—they just chase everyone else and try to kick balls out. Once a player loses their ball, they too become monsters. Very fast paced and great for learning to hold the ball.

Numbers: Heads up dribbling. Everyone has a ball and dribbles in confined space. Coaches stand in various places and periodically hold up fingers. Kids try to be the first to scream out the number of fingers held up. With multiple coaches, this really helps kids look around in all directions and keep their heads up when dribbling.

Follow the Leader: Heads up and creative dribbling. Pair up players. In each pair, one player is the leader and the other follows as the leader dribbles around varying speed, direction, and moves that the follower should mimic.

Passing

Random Goals: Heads up passing, teamwork, movement without the ball. Set up 8-12 small goals with cones randomly in a 20x30 yd space. Pair up players with one ball per pair. Each pair tries to pass their ball through a goal and to their partner, then moves on to another goal. Coaches can move about with a "moving goal" made of a rope or pole carried by two adults. 1 point for each regular goal, 3 for the moving goal. Play for about 1 minute and see how many points each pair can score.

> A note on using scoring in drills—rather than compare scores among teams and setting goals the weaker pairs cannot reach, simply ask kids to see if they can beat their personal best in the next round. This helps all players improve at their own level.

Short-short-long: Passing technique work. Three players in a line with one ball. The player at one end push passes short to a player in the middle about 10 yards away. The middle player passes short back to the first player, who then passes long to the third player who is 20 yds away. This player controls the ball, passes short to the middle player, back to the 3rd player, then long to the first player and on and on.

Keepaway Circle: Passing and trapping skills, defending, socializing. Teams at all levels do this as a warm up. Have most players in a circle with 2 in the middle as defenders. The outside players try to pass the ball around without hitting it out of the circle or letting the defenders touch it. If the ball goes out or is touched by a defender, the player hitting the pass switches with a defender who joins the outside circle. The smaller the circle or the less touches allowed by the outside players, the harder this is. Surprisingly fun and social and skill demanding.

4 Box: Passing, movement, spacing. Set up a grid divided into 4 15x15 boxes. Have teams of 4 in each box with a ball for each team. Start off with a team passing the ball in their box making sure they are moving to get open and all players touch the ball. Once they are comfortable with this, have them move after passing to the next box and work clockwise through the boxes as a team. So the first player passes to a teammate and moves to box 2, the receiving player passes to a third player and then moves to box 2 (and spreads out away from her teammate). The third player passes to the last player, and moves to the 2nd box, where the last player plays the ball into box 2 to one of the 3 teammates already there. Each team rotates through the 4 boxes back

to their home box. Work on increasing the speed of play and spacing in the box.

3 v. 1 Box Drill: Set up a 10x10 box, with 3 offensive players each in one corner, the ball with the player in the middle. One defender is in the middle of the box. The player with the ball passes "square" to a player in one adjacent corner. The non-receiving player runs to the open corner, giving the receiving player two options in the new adjacent corners. Keep this up until the defender touches the ball or an errant pass leaves the box. Make the offensive player who made the bad pass switch with the defender.

Keep-away: Two teams of equal numbers, each team tries to keep the ball away from the other as long as possible. Playing without any boundaries encourages kids to look for open spaces. You can add scoring with a goal for 5 passes in a row. One of the best ways to teach spacing and thinking a couple passes ahead.

Pavlovian Points Scored Scrimmage: A good follow-up to Keep-away to move tactically into more regular play is to play a scrimmage with regular goals but still aim for players to spread out and move the ball. A scoring system can encourage quality play, such as awarding a point for each back pass, a point for switching the ball from one side to the other, a point for 5 consecutive passes, a point for passing wide to an alley 10 yrs from the touchline, and a point for scoring an actual goal. 10 points wins a game, first team to win three games wins the set. This is an amazingly effective way to manipulate quality play without a lot of direction from the coach. The kids are like trained seals in following the scoring system. Add in points for any particular skill you are targeting.

Using Width: (See diagram below): Create a field with 2 alleys on wings. Place extra player(s) in the alleys who are undefended outlets for the teams playing on the field. The job of these touchline wing players is to be available for receiving passes and playing a good return pass to the same team. Wings can't go out of alley but can move up and down field to support. Great for teaching spreading out the field and helping kids learn not to panic and just kick the ball away, knowing there is always someone open for a safe pass.

Shooting

Line-ups: Teaches striking the ball and shot placement. There are all sorts of ways of having a line of kids who pass the ball to the coach from about 18 yards out and the coach drops off a return pass for the player to run onto and shoot on goal. Kids like these although it involves a bit of waiting.

Kick the Coach: Once kids have learned shooting technique, set up a 20x20 box, with each player with a ball. Have them chase you and try to hit the coach with shots. You can get real laughs by having some punishment if you get hit X number of times (like push-ups or the chicken dance or imitating a giraffe).

World Cup: Quick release of shots. Everyone but the goalie is in front of the goal and trying to score. You throw out one ball and whoever hits it in the goal is done and leaves the field (this is a great way to end practice). Throw out another ball or even a couple at a time and let the kids all work to score. Everyone scores eventually, feels successful, and has fun (except maybe the goalie).

Lines Behind the Goal: Works on dribbling, defending, and shooting. Get two lines of players behind the goal with the goalie in goal. The coach stands near the goal with a pile of balls. Throw or kick the ball out 15-30 yards and the front players from each line chase it and then play 1 v 1 to try to score. If one player loses the ball, the other player is on offense right away. After the ball goes out of bounds or scores, the next two front players go 1 v 1 for the next ball you throw out. You can vary the numbers to 2 v 2 or more (or even All v All). Kids love this one, work hard, and get to watch their teammates fight it out. Can be a good prelude to scrimmage time.

Small field shoot at will: Shooting from distance, with quickness. One of my fondest memories from college practice was when we played with full teams on a 40 yard field with full size goals. Basically, a good shooter could score from anywhere on the field. If you were open, you shoot. Good to get kids shooting from distance and not being afraid to "give it a try."

Small Sided Games

3 v. 3: In college, we played 3 v. 3 more than anything else we did. This is a microcosm of full field soccer where much of the time your options with the ball involve 2 other players nearby. Played on a small field, maybe the size of the penalty box, 3 v. 3 requires working hard to get open, to pass and trap skillfully, and to find small openings to try to score. Can be made more challenging by playing one touch or two touch or making x number of passes count as a goal. With younger kids, 4 v. 4 or 5 v. 5 can be just as useful.

On organizing teams: For small sides, I like to divide the team into groups that have enough for two "subteams" for whatever size teams I want to use. So if we will play 4 v. 4, I make groups of 8 and let them divide into 2 teams of 4. Then as we play round robin against other teams, the aggregate score of your two teams is what determines the "champion." This lets the kids strategize on how to make their two groups, and makes the overall result less dependent on any one small group or player.

1-2-3-4-5: Two teams of equal numbers, one ball, unlimited space. Each player on each team assigned a different sequential number, so there are two 1's, two 2's etc. 1 passes to 2, 2 to 3, etc, with 5 (or whatever is last number) passing to 1. You can only cover your own number (1 covers 1). If the ball is turned over, whoever gets it passes it to their next number. Teaches moving to get open, anticipating the next play, working with your teammates, and passing to space.

4 <u>Goals</u>: Small sided game with two goals for each team. Set up either in both corners on each end or goals at each midpoint (see drawing below). This leads kids to change the field, look up, and spread out.

5 v. 5 v. 5: This is basically half field soccer. One team is offense and one defense (the defensive team should designate a goalie, so it is 5 v. 4 on the field. The third 5 person team waits in the goal at the opposite end of the field. When the defense gets the ball, if they can get the ball across midfield, they are on offense on the other end of the field and the waiting team becomes the new defense. The first offensive team goes to wait in the goal they were attacking, becoming the next defensive team when the ball gets back in their half of the field. This all seems quite relaxing at first with all the waiting in the goal, but it becomes very fast paced and tiring after about 3 end changes. One of the most "game-like" drills I know.

<u>Scrimmage Restrictions</u>: There are countless stipulations you can make in scrimmaging that can help players develop their soccer sense. A few used most often include:

Passing: Require a certain number of passes before shooting. Or count a certain number of passes as a goal. For example, make each team make five passes before shooting. Or maybe 8 (or 10) passes counts as a goal.

Pushing Up: To score, every player on a team has to be in the offensive half of the field. Helps defenders learn to push up and get involved in supporting the offense.

Backpassing: Every third pass needs to be a backpass, or before a team shoots, they must make at least one back pass.

Multiple goals: Use full size goals (with goalies) at the end lines and small goals at midfield (with no goalies). Each team has two goals to attack and the other two to defend. This can really help teach vision and switching fields as players switch their attack from the big goal and swing the ball around to the midfield goal suddenly.

Switching fields: Stipulate that the ball must go within 15 yards of both sidelines before you can shoot on goal.

Limited touches: Have teams play three or two or one touch. This eliminates dribbling and kids holding the ball too long, teaches kids to think ahead and to support each other. One touch is very advanced but a common technique for top-level teams.

Selfless talk: Tell your players they cannot call for the ball in scrimmage but can only say where the player with the ball should pass it. This lessens the tendency for everyone to yell for the ball to be passed to them (usually even when they are not open) and increases the kind of team communication to help players think a step or two ahead.

Progressive Activities
Below are some activities that flow smoothly from one to another and can involve all the players at a practice. Once you set up the stations, there is a momentum to having a series of connected and purposeful activities.

Circuit Course: Usually we do this with players in pairs and the proper equipment at each station. Use a set a time (usually about 30 seconds) for each station. A lot of these exercises can be used to build core strength in addition to ball skills.

Touches on top of ball
Pushups
Sit-ups
Squat thrusts
Jumping jacks
Jump over ball
Juggling on body parts (head, thigh, foot)
Piggyback Walk
Planks
Jump rope or hula-hoop

Relay Races (always fun): Make teams of 3-6 players (if you get more than this there is too much waiting around).

Dribble forward and back
Dribble backward and back
Dribble up, leave ball, run back (next person runs up, dribbles back)
Dribble up and pass ball back
Slalom course dribbling around cones
Sprint up and back
Piggyback up and back
All together up and back

Olympics: Teams (of 5-10 players) compete for high score. Each event is a separate competition and scoring adds up for the team total. Some of these are one off events and others, such as juggling, you give the players a set time (maybe 3 minutes) to see what the highest score they can get. Having a scorekeeper for each team can help this run more quickly and smoothly.

Lap Run: Top finishers get points (10 for first, 9 for second…1 for 10th).
Big Box Cone Knocking: Pairs of players lined up about 15-20 yards apart with cones midway between lines of players. They

pass back and forth and try to hit the cones as they pass across to each other. (1 point for each cone hit).

Individual Juggle (highest number achieved without the ball hitting the ground: 15 point maximum).

Pairs Juggle (highest number achieved without the ball hitting the ground).

Team Juggle (# of diff people times 2).

Pairs heading (highest number achieved without the ball hitting the ground).

Pairs kicking, steps away: Have pairs 20-40 yards apart. Each person kicks 5 times to the other and each time the receiving player counts how many giant steps she has to take to receive the pass. This really emphasizes accuracy. Low scores are better here, so you can give 10 points for any pair with less than 10 steps, and take off 1 point for every step over 10 (11 steps would get a score of 9, 12 steps, 8, 20 steps would get 1 point).

Passing between two cones: Players in pairs with 2 cones making an alley halfway between them. Each pass through the cones scores a point.

Longest throw (10 for first, 9 for second...1 for 10th).

Hula Hoop Chip (accuracy) (1 point for every ball hit into a hula hoop).

Penalty shots: This is a good final or second to final event. 1 point for each goal scored.

Slalom Race Dribbling: Set up cones in slalom pattern for dribbling up and back. A good final event where you might give the leading team a head start (maybe 1 second for every point ahead). Relay race style where each player dribbles up and back. The first team done wins!

Warm-up

Dynamic Stretching: There are all sorts of reasons static stretching (standing still and touching toes, rotating upper body, etc.) is less worthwhile than dynamic stretching (stretching while moving). Most importantly, dynamic stretching is more fun for kids. Pro teams do this and look really cool and intimidating as they march around the perimeter of the field in two parallel lines following the leader with knee lifts, heels to butt, sideways shuffle, grapevine, etc. For younger players, I usually have them line up on an endline with another line of cones about 10-15 yards away and shout out the direction for the next warm-up. Soon enough, a player can take charge of this as the leader. These are warm-ups, not races, so everything should be done at low speeds. The possibilities are endless of what to do; here are a few described.

Jog up and back
Run backwards up and back
Sideways shuffle (face the same direction up and back to get both sides stretched)
Grapevine: Sideways shuffle with crossed feet
Pick the flowers: Reach down and pick grass every other step
Skipping
Hop on one foot
Goalkeeper leaps: Like skipping but reaching high to catch imaginary high ball
Sprint up and jog back (to get heart rate up after earlier, easier stretches)
Butt kicks: Jog forward and kick heels to butt
Knee lifts: Skip but with lifting one knee up toward chest

Three Person Continuous Warm-up: I learned this from Bobby Clarke at Stanford. Players are put in groups of 3 and set up about 20 yards apart with two players at one end with one ball and the third at the other end. As the player with the ball does some skill drill, the others are doing their own stretching as they wait for their turn with the ball. So player 1 dribbles with her right foot down to player 2 who dribbles with his right foot back to player 3 who dribbles with his right foot back to player 1. Then player 1 dribbles with her left foot to player 2 to player 3. Then player 1 scoots the ball with the bottom of her foot forwards to 2 to 3, then maybe pull the ball with the bottom of the foot backwards.... You can add all sorts of dribbling skill tricks into this warm-up and the players get stretching in as they work on skill development. This can easily move into passing drills where player 1 passes to player 2 and follows her pass across, player 2 passes to 3 and follows, etc. This just keeps flowing as long as you have another skill to work on.

CPSIA information can be obtained at www.ICGtesting.com
Printed in the USA
LVOW10s1610110416

483077LV00050B/1982/P